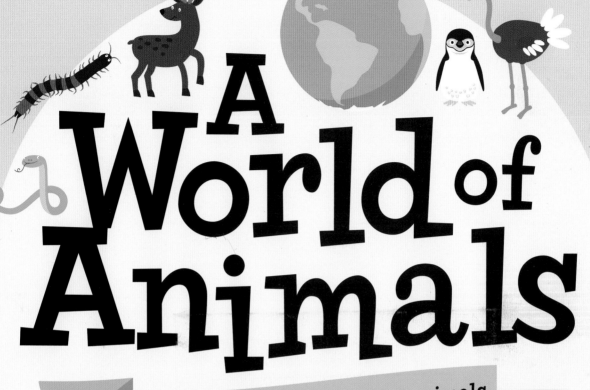

A World of Animals

Learn to draw more than 175 animals
from the seven continents!

Walter Foster
Jr.

Illustrated by Rimma Zainagova

Brimming with creative inspiration, how-to projects, and useful information to enrich your everyday life, Quarto Knows is a favorite destination for those pursuing their interests and passions. Visit our site and dig deeper with our books into your area of interest: Quarto Creates, Quarto Cooks, Quarto Homes, Quarto Lives, Quarto Drives, Quarto Explores, Quarto Gifts, or Quarto Kids.

Published by Walter Foster Publishing,
an imprint of Quarto Publishing Group USA Inc.

First published in 2021 by Walter Foster Jr., an imprint of The Quarto Group.
26391 Crown Valley Parkway, Suite 220, Mission Viejo, CA 92691, USA.
T (949) 380-7510 F (949) 380-7575 **www.QuartoKnows.com**

Walter Foster Jr. titles are also available at discount for retail, wholesale, promotional, and bulk purchase. For details, contact the Special Sales Manager by email at specialsales@quarto.com or by mail at The Quarto Group, Attn: Special Sales Manager, 100 Cummings Center, Suite 265D, Beverly, MA 01915, USA.

ISBN: 978-1-60058-878-5

Digital edition published in 2020
eISBN: 978-1-60058-879-2

Illustrations by Rimma Zainagova.
Step-by-step artwork by Paul Calver.

Printed in China
10 9 8 7 6 5 4 3 2 1

Contents

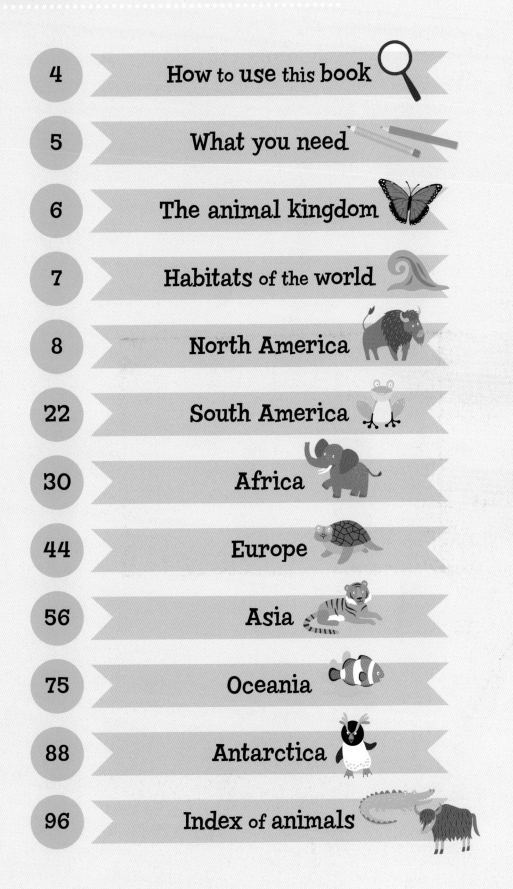

How to use this book

This book is packed with information and colorful illustrations of animals, as well as more than 40 stickers, 176 step-by-step drawing projects, and a two-sided poster. One side of the poster is a world map showing which animals are found where; the other side features a continent-by-continent guide to the animal kingdom.

The book is divided into seven chapters. Each chapter covers the wildlife of a particular continent.

Name of continent and information about it.

Location of continent on a map of the world.

Illustration, animal name, and information about that animal.

Position the correct sticker on the animal information pages.

Animal sticker

Description of some important habitats in each continent.

Grayed-out animal silhouettes to find and complete with the correct sticker.

The world map poster showing the main geographic location of each animal.

An illustrated continent-by-continent guide to world wildlife.

What you need

Alongside the animal information, stickers, and poster are step-by-step lessons showing how to draw every unique creature in this book. To create your own gallery of animals, grab a pencil and some paper; then follow each step, adding the details as you draw. When you are finished, add color with crayons, markers, or paints if you like! Here are the tools and materials you will need:

pencil sharpener

eraser

paper

drawing pencil

coloring pencils

marker pens

paintbrush

paints

The animal kingdom

Scientists estimate that there are 1.25 million different species of animals on Earth. Because some species are similar to others, they can be grouped together. One group is invertebrates (animals without a backbone); the other is vertebrates (animals with a backbone). The vertebrates are divided into five groups: fish, amphibians, reptiles, birds, and mammals.

Invertebrates

More than 97 percent of all animals do not have a backbone. The invertebrates include insects, crustaceans (like crabs), spiders, mollusks (like squid), worms, and jellyfish.

Fish

These aquatic animals breathe underwater through gills. They have fins and most have scales. Most fish lay eggs. There are 32,000 species of fish.

Amphibians

Amphibian means "double life," as these animals can live in water and on land. Most amphibians lay eggs. There are 8,000 species.

Reptiles

Reptiles include snakes, lizards, crocodiles, turtles, and tortoises. Their skin is scaly, covered with hard bony plates or a mixture of both. There are more than 11,000 species.

Birds

These warm-blooded animals have feathers and wings, and most can fly. They all lay eggs. They evolved alongside the dinosaurs. There are 10,000 bird species.

Mammals

These warm-blooded animals have lungs and breathe air. They have hair or fur and feed their young with milk. There are 5,000 species. Humans are mammals.

Habitats of the world

The natural home of an animal is its habitat. Here, an animal will find the food, drink, and shelter it needs. The habitats of some animals are vast; others are very small. Many species may share one habitat. Below are the 12 main habitats on Earth.

Grasslands

The plants dominating this often flat, open habitat are grasses. There are few trees. Grasslands, also known as savannas and prairies, cover a quarter of the planet.

Coniferous forest

Dominated by evergreen needle-leaved pine, fir, and larch trees, these forests are found in cold polar regions and all the way through to the warmer tropics.

Still freshwater

Standing freshwater in wetlands, swamps, bogs, and some lakes is the perfect habitat for many animals, especially small and juvenile invertebrates.

Deserts

A desert receives less than 10 inches of rain a year. Not all deserts are hot—some are very cold, even polar and ice-covered! There are sandy and rocky deserts.

Mountains

From base to tip, there are woodlands, forests, meadows, lakes and streams, tundra, and exposed rock. It gets colder at higher elevations.

Oceans and seas

Three-quarters of the Earth's surface is saltwater, but most remains unexplored. Habitats range from sunlit, tropical shallows to dark, cold depths of 12,000 feet.

Rainforests

More than 160 inches of rain falls a year in a rainforest. Thousands of species find a home between the shaded floor and the towering green canopy.

Polar regions

This habitat is treeless, and temperatures drop to below freezing for most of the year. The surface may be frozen soil or covered with ice. In winter, the poles are in darkness.

Shoreline and coasts

Tides, waves, and wind mean that animals in this habitat, which includes mangrove swamps, are adapted to its consistently changing conditions.

Temperate forests

The broad-leaved trees, mosses, and ferns in this habitat get generous rain. Also known as woodlands, they change with the four seasons.

Moving freshwater

Moving freshwater in rivers, streams, and some lakes suits animals that require high oxygen levels or to have their food "delivered" to them.

Coral reefs

Found near tropical oceans and seas in depths of up to 150 feet, sun-soaked reefs are rich in both permanent and visiting marine and bird life.

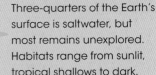

North America

North America is the world's third-largest continent. Diverse habitats—including ice and tundra, forests, grasslands, deserts, wetlands, and sandy coastlines—and climates support a wide range of wildlife. The gila monster, black bear, American alligator, bison, and bald eagle are among the animals unique to North America.

Where in the world

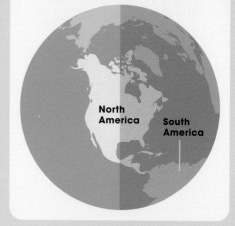

North America

South America

Key habitats

Rocky Mountains
Its snow-capped peaks, rocky terrain, forests, grasslands, and rivers are a haven for wildlife.

Mojave Desert
With temperatures of 8°F to 120°F and low rainfall, this dry desert is home to many reptiles and mammals.

Lake Superior
Lake Superior is, by surface area, the largest lake in the world. More than 80 fish species live in its clear, clean water.

The Everglades
More than 70 threatened species are found in this wetland. It is the only place alligators and crocodiles coexist!

The animals

Bald eagle
Bald eagles have a white head and tail and a brown body. They can spot a rabbit from two miles away.

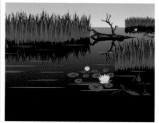

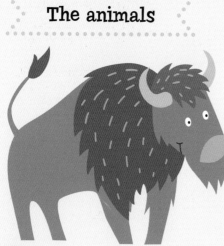

Bison
Herds of bison, standing six feet tall, roam grassy plains. Shaggy fur keeps them warm in cold winters. In summer, they shed their coats.

Beaver
Beavers build dams to create a pond of calm water in which they can build their stick and mud lodges.

Moose
Male moose use their antlers to show dominance in the mating season. The antlers are cast off in the summer.

Arctic fox

Arctic foxes live in underground dens. They have brown fur in the summer and grow thick white coats for the harsh Arctic winters.

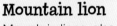

Brown pelican

The pouch below the brown pelican's bill can hold up to three gallons of water.

Monarch butterfly

Monarchs make a 3,000-mile winter migration south. Their wingspan is four inches.

Ptarmigan

Ptarmigans are small birds that prefer frozen regions. Their plumage is white in winter.

Mountain lion

Mountain lions, also known as panthers, pumas, or cougars, are hunters that eat elk and rabbits.

Caribbean reef shark

Found along the Atlantic Ocean coast from Florida to Brazil, this reef shark grows to 10 feet and feeds on bony fish.

California newt

Newts can live for 15 years. Their warty skin produces a toxin that can kill or paralyze a predator.

Bighorn sheep

Named for their large horns, these sheep can climb steep, rocky slopes with speed and ease.

Alligator

Alligators are strong and fierce reptiles that can grow to 11 feet long. Alligators have wide, round snouts.

Desert tarantula

These large, hairy spiders hunt at night for insects, other spiders, small lizards, and mice.

Black bear

Black bears mostly feed on vegetation, but will eat fish and mammals. Coat colors include red, blond, and blue.

Gila monster

These large reptiles live in hot deserts. They are one of the few lizards that have a venomous bite.

Elephant seal

Northern elephant seals have a large nose. They can hold their breath underwater for up to two hours while hunting for fish.

Arctic ground squirrel

These squirrels live in burrows dug three feet below the tundra. They hibernate from September to April.

Sea otter

Sea otters eat, sleep, mate, and give birth in water. They feed on shellfish, fish, and squid.

Polar bear

Polar bears have black skin, and their outer hairs are transparent. Seals are their main food.

Resplendent quetzal

These brightly colored birds live in mountainous tropical forests. Only males have the long, trailing tail feathers.

Green toad

These secretive toads spend most of their time in burrows, often only emerging after rainfall.

Giant desert centipede

This desert- and seashore-dwelling centipede grows to eight inches. It is a carnivore.

Basking shark

These 32-foot gentle giants eat with their mouths wide open to filter plankton from the water.

Narwhal

Male narwhals' tusks grow to six feet long. The tusk is a tooth in the upper jaw. Narwhals are whales.

Snowy owl

These stealthy hunters can eat more than 1,600 lemmings in a year. Hedwig in "Harry Potter" is a snowy owl.

Walrus

Walruses use their tusks for cutting ice holes, defense, and hauling themselves out from the water.

Brown bear

These big bears eat berries, roots, small mammals, fish, and decaying dead animals.

Snowy owl

Walrus

Monarch butterfly

Brown pelican

1

2

3

4

Bald eagle

1

2

3

4

5

Gila monster

1

2

3

4

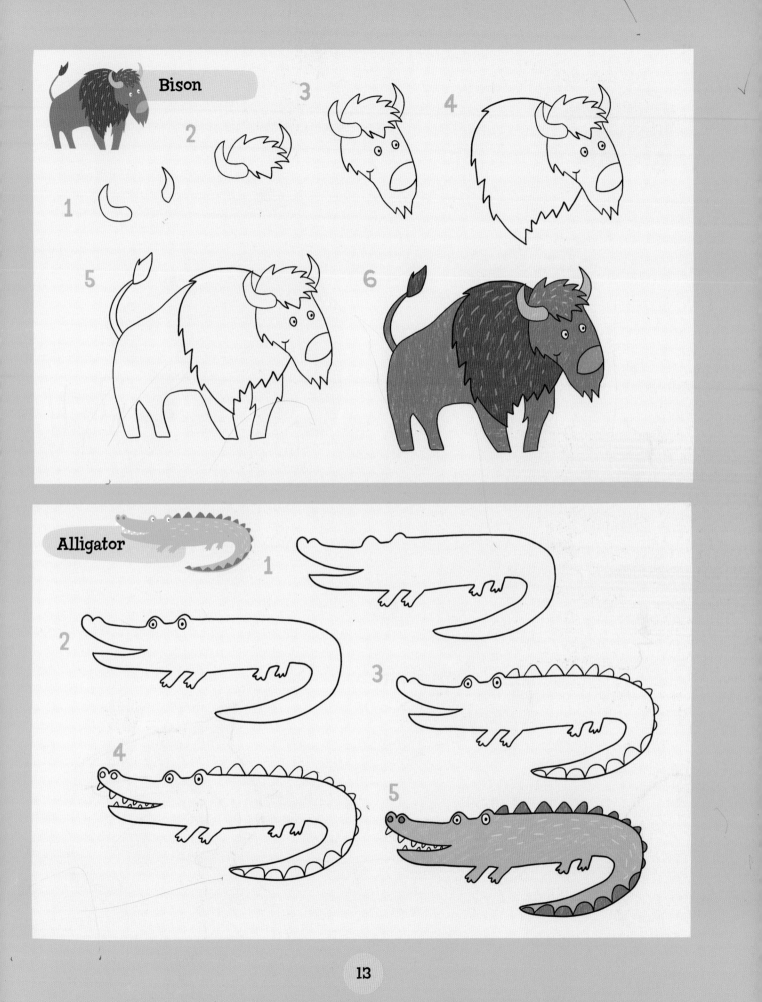

Bison

1 2 3 4 5 6

Alligator

1 2 3 4 5

Black bear

Caribbean reef shark

Desert tarantula

Mountain lion

Resplendent quetzal

Basking shark

1

2

3

4

Brown bear

1

2

3

4

5

16

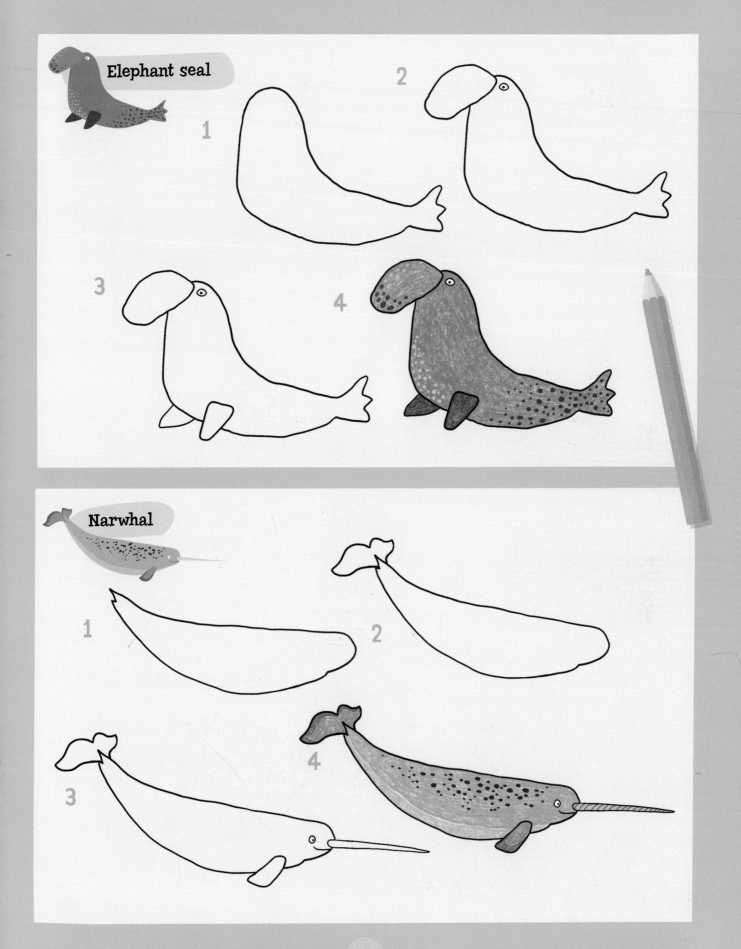

Elephant seal

1

2

3

4

Narwhal

1

2

3

4

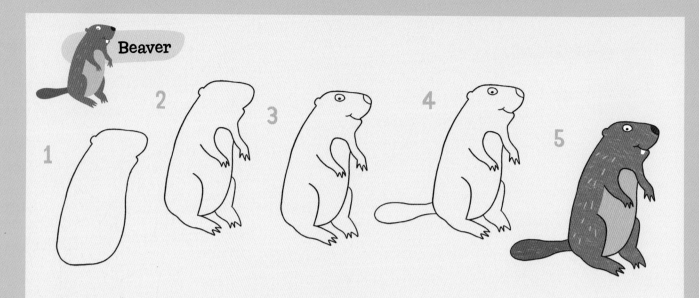

Beaver

1 2 3 4 5

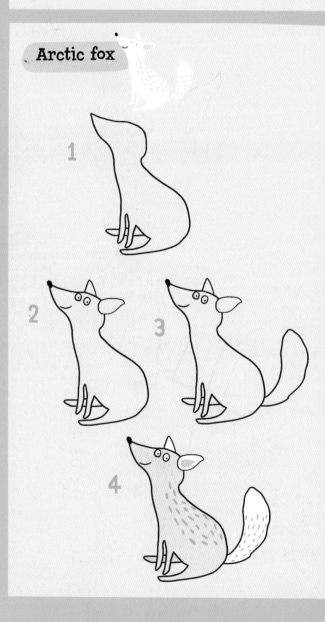

Arctic fox

1
2
3
4

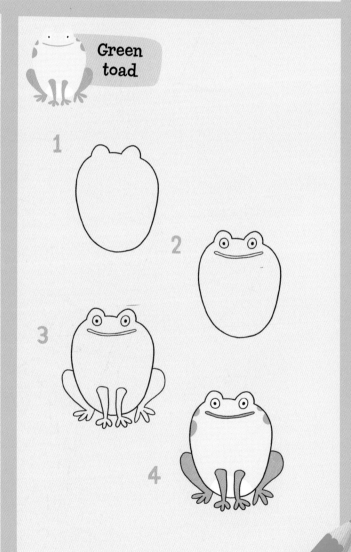

Green toad

1
2
3
4

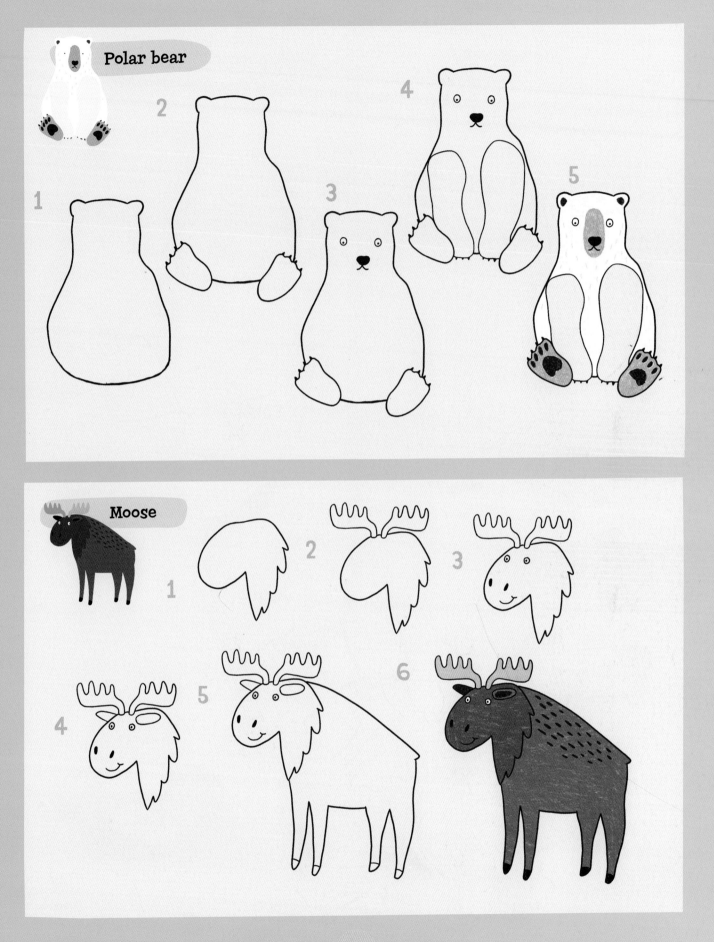

Polar bear

1

2

3

4

5

Moose

1

2

3

4

5

6

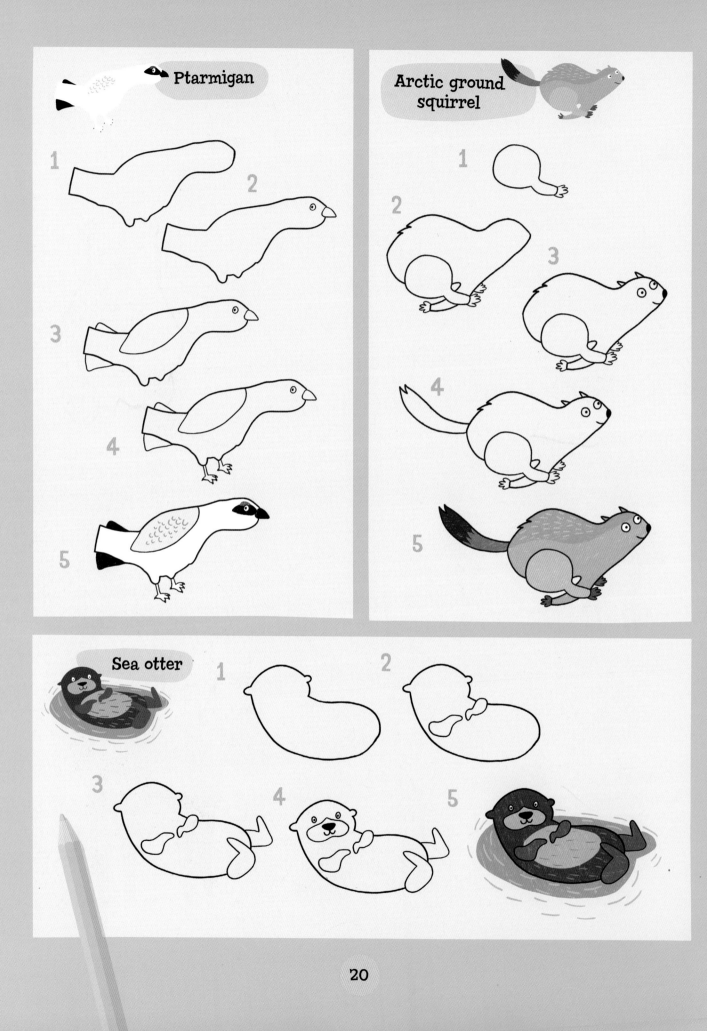

Ptarmigan

1
2
3
4
5

Arctic ground squirrel

1
2
3
4
5

Sea otter

1
2
3
4
5

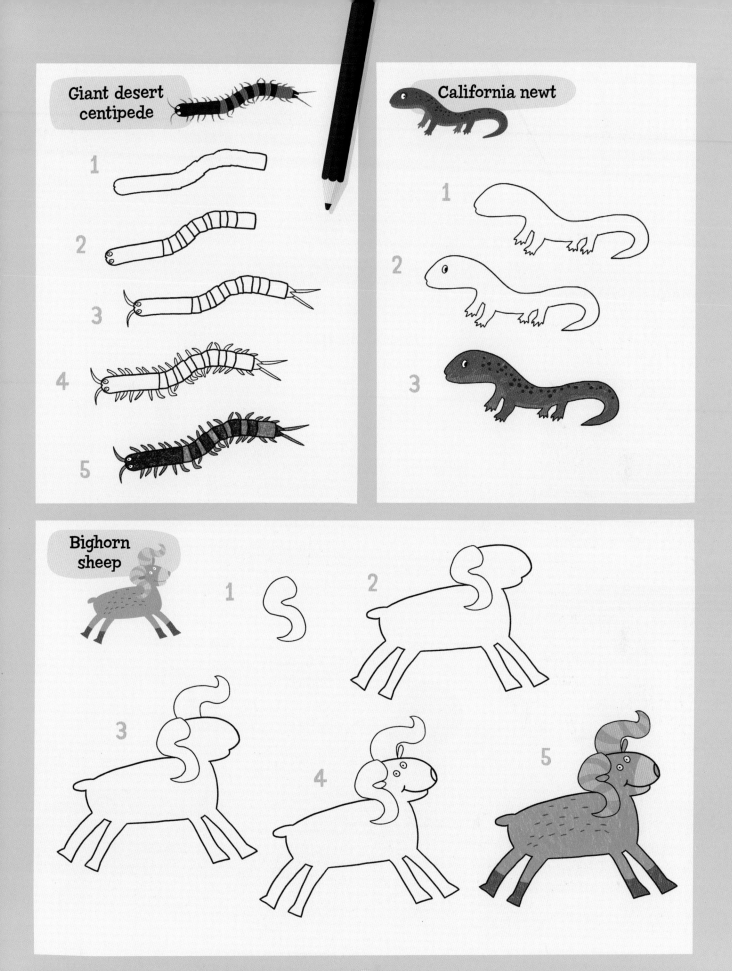

Giant desert centipede

1

2

3

4

5

California newt

1

2

3

Bighorn sheep

1

2

3

4

5

South America

South America is an important continent for the study of animals and their habitats. Of special note for their unique wildlife are the Galapagos Islands and the Amazon Rainforest. Most of the continent is tropical rainforests and forests, but there are deserts, wetlands, grasslands (pampas), and snow-capped mountainous regions.

Where in the world

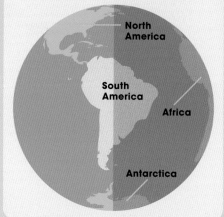

North America

South America

Africa

Antarctica

Key habitats

The Amazon
Equal in size to the lower 48 states of the USA, this vast rainforest has 10 million animal and plant species.

The Andes
These mountains run the length of the continent's west coast, and 1,000 fauna species live on its plateaus and peaks.

The Pantanal
The world's largest wetland, the Pantanal, floods in the wet season and empties in the dry season.

Monteverde Forest
This cloud forest of swamps, woodlands, and rainforests is often covered by low-level clouds.

The animals

Andean condor
With a wingspan of 10 feet, condors are one of the world's largest flying birds. They scavenge carrion (dead animals).

Llama
Llamas are related to camels. Humans use them to carry heavy loads on their backs and for their wool. They eat grass.

Emerald tree boa
These snakes lie in wait on a tree branch, and when a small rodent passes below, they strike.

Flamingo
Four flamingo species live in South America. The pink plumage results from their diet of algae and invertebrates.

Poison dart frog

Colorful poison dart frogs measure 0.6 to 2.5 inches. One species has enough venom to kill 10 adults.

Giant armadillo

These insect eaters spent most of their lives underground and only come up at night.

Sloth

Sloths live in trees and eat twigs, leaves, and buds. In a day, they sleep for up to 20 hours and move only 40 yards.

Blue morpho butterfly

Their large wings are vivid blue on top and brown underneath. The morpho feeds on decaying fruit.

Flying tree frog

These rainforest and forest frogs can glide up to 50 feet through the air with help from their webbed feet and skin flaps.

Pudu

Pudus are very small deer that stand just 15 inches tall. These solitary animals are herbivores.

Giant anteater

To get their daily diet of 35,000 ants, toothless anteaters tear ant hills apart with their claws and stick their snout and sticky tongue inside.

Galapagos penguin

These are the most northerly of all penguins. They zip through water at up to 21 mph when chasing fish.

Toucan

The sharp, serrated edge on their huge, colorful bills peels the fruits that toucans eat.

Piranha

Piranhas live in freshwater rivers and lakes. Their razor-sharp, interlocking teeth suit their mostly meat and fish diet.

Magnificent frigatebird

Males of this species have a striking red throat pouch. They inflate it to attract a mate.

Jaguar

These big cats are good swimmers, so they eat turtles and fish in addition to land animals.

Galapagos giant tortoise

The oldest giant tortoise lived 170 years, but in the wild 100 years is more usual. Between long naps, they eat vegetation.

Let's learn to draw!

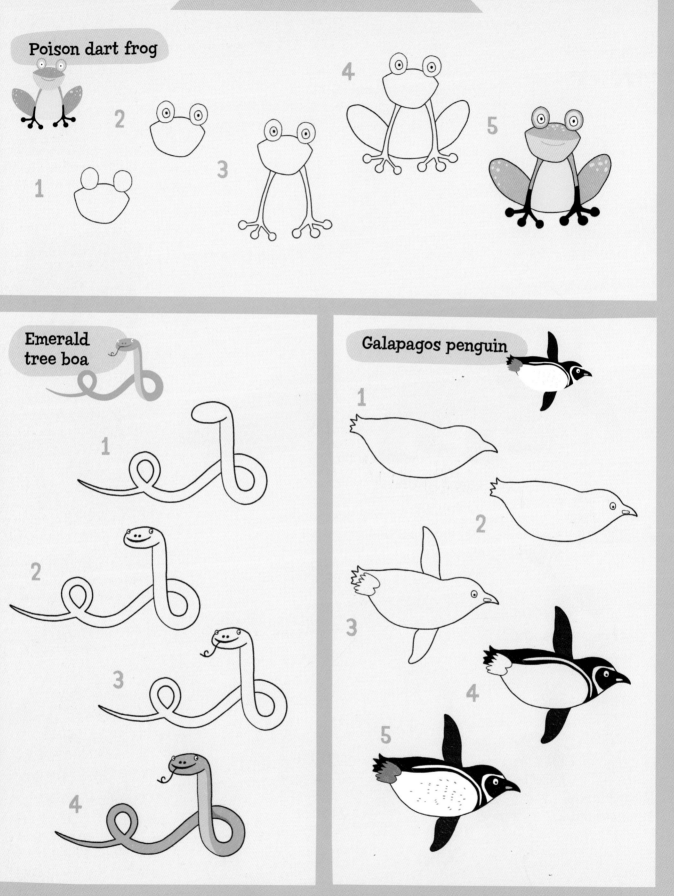

Poison dart frog

1 2 3 4 5

Emerald tree boa

1 2 3 4

Galapagos penguin

1 2 3 4 5

Sloth

1

2

3

4

5

Magnificent frigatebird

1

2

3

4

5

Flamingo

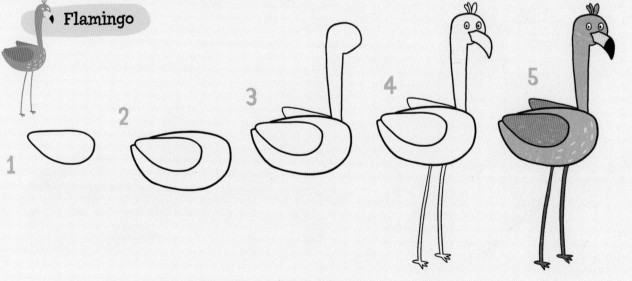

1

2

3

4

5

Andean condor

1
2
3
4
5
6

Flying tree frog

1
2
3
4
5

Galapagos giant tortoise

1
2
3
4
5
6

Llama

Giant armadillo

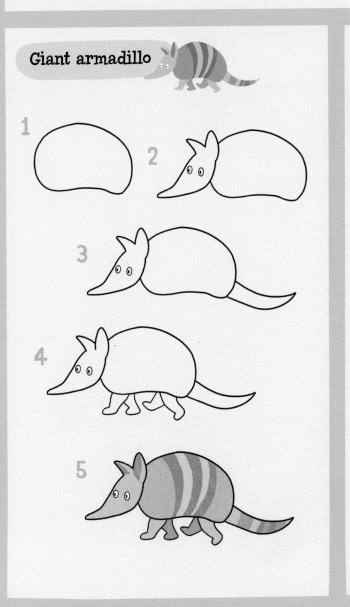

Piranha

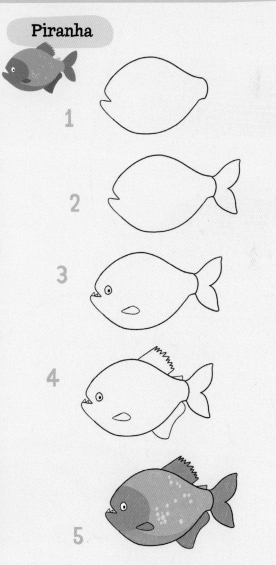

Jaguar

1

2

3

4

Giant anteater

1

2

3

4

Pudu

Blue morpho
butterfly

Toucan

Africa

The huge continent of Africa is home to some amazing wildlife and extreme habitats. The scorching heat of the Sahara Desert is one of the harshest places for animals to survive, while other creatures thrive in steamy rainforests. Then, there are the open grasslands that are home to the world's largest herds of grazing animals.

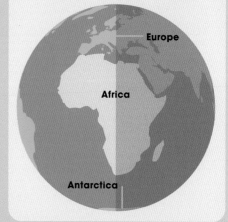

Europe

Africa

Antarctica

Key habitats

Kruger National Park
Grasslands, dense bush, and flat terrain make this park a haven for elephants, lions, rhinos, and more.

Sahara Desert
This desert is the same size as the USA, and there are dunes, salt flats, gravel plains, and mountains.

Nile River
The Nile is more than 4,000 miles long. Its water and fertile banks attract fish, hippos, reptiles, and birds.

Congo Basin
Its rainforests, grasslands, rivers, flooded forests, and swamps are teeming with wildlife, some endangered.

The animals

Chameleon
Chameleons are famous for being able to change their skin color and seeing in two directions at once.

Ostrich
Ostriches are the world's largest birds. Although they can't fly, they can run 44 mph.

Zebra
Each zebra has a unique pattern of stripes, which may confuse predators and act as camouflage.

Western gorilla
These large and powerful gorillas live in troops of five to 30 individuals. A male silverback leads the troop.

Chimpanzee

Chimpanzees sleep in trees but forage for food on the ground during the day,

Great white shark

These sharks are fierce predators. Their mouths contain 300 sharp teeth arranged in up to seven rows.

Leopard

Leopards are strong enough to haul dead deer and pigs up into tree branches.

Goliath frog

The world's largest frogs can grow to 12.5 inches and jump 10 feet. They do not croak.

Black rhinoceros

The horns on black rhinos grow throughout their lives. These mammals are plant-eaters.

Lion

Though known as "the king of the jungle," most lions live in grasslands.

Ring-tailed lemur

Ring-tailed lemurs are unique to Madagascar. Their striped tails are longer than their bodies!

Giraffe

Everything about giraffes is long: 16-feet tall with six-feet tall legs, and a 21-inch tongue,

Giant African land snail

These snails, with their seven-inch shells, thrive in hot and humid conditions.

Hippopotamus

Hippos spend 16 hours a day in the water, and they can hold their breath for five minutes.

Dung beetle

These beetles are nature's recyclers. They move, bury, live in, and eat other animals' poop!

African elephant

These elephants are the world's largest land mammal. The huge ears of these herbivores help radiate excess body heat.

Baboon
Baboons live in grasslands, scrub, and forests. They are omnivores, so they eat meat and vegetation.

Mudskipper
These amphibious fish can breathe on land and in water. They get around on land using their modified fins.

Horned desert viper
To avoid daytime heat and to ambush prey, these venomous snakes burrow into sand.

Camel
Dromedary camels have only one hump, and they can go 10 days without water.

Giant manta ray
Giant mantas can grow to 29 feet across. They swim with their mouths open to filter plankton from the water.

Dugong
Dugongs are also called sea cows because the only thing they eat is long, narrow seagrass leaves.

Caracal
These wild cats with long black tufts on their ears are active at night when it is cool. They will eat any animal they can catch.

Steppe eagle
These raptors have a wide distribution, from Russia through to South Africa.

Whale shark
These sharks grow to 45 feet. Their gills filter plankton and small fish from 1,600 gallons of water an hour.

Walia ibex
These wild goats roam slippery and very steep, rocky cliffs, eating the sparse vegetation.

Let's learn to draw!

Chameleon

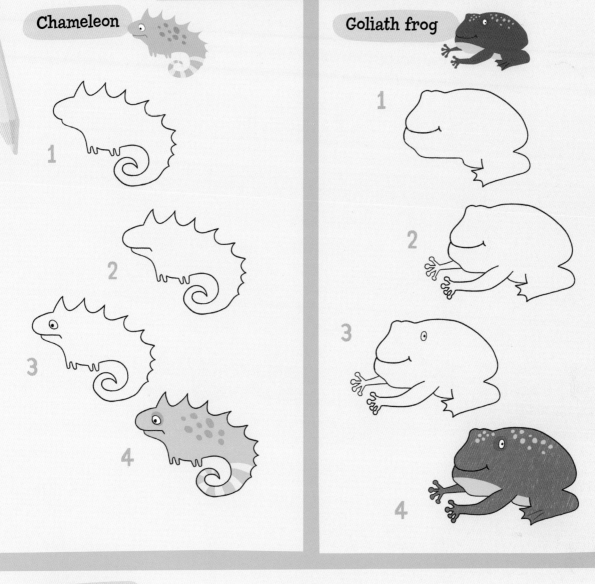

Goliath frog

Ring-tailed lemur

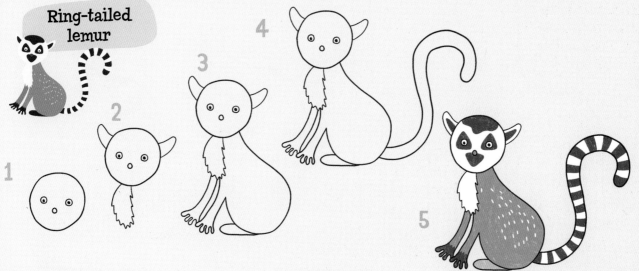

33

African elephant

Giraffe

34

Mudskipper

Chimpanzee

Giant African land snail

35

Zebra

1
2
3
4
5

Horned desert viper

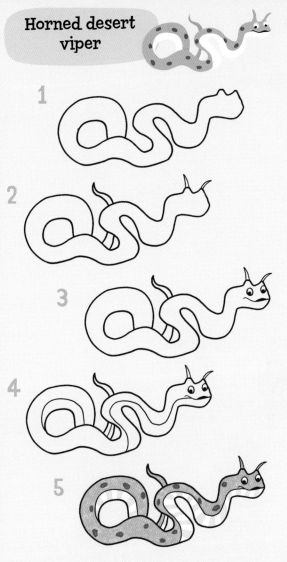

1
2
3
4
5

Ostrich

1
2
3
4
5
6

Leopard

Dung beetle

Caracal

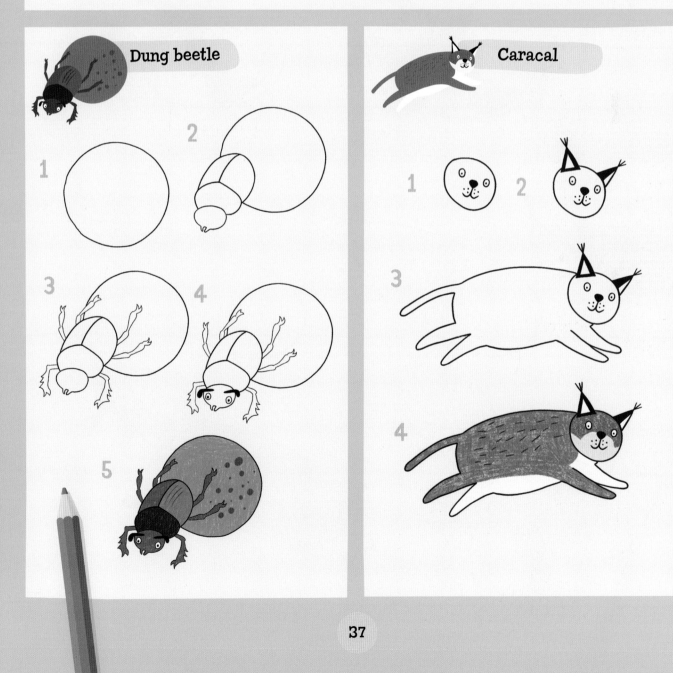

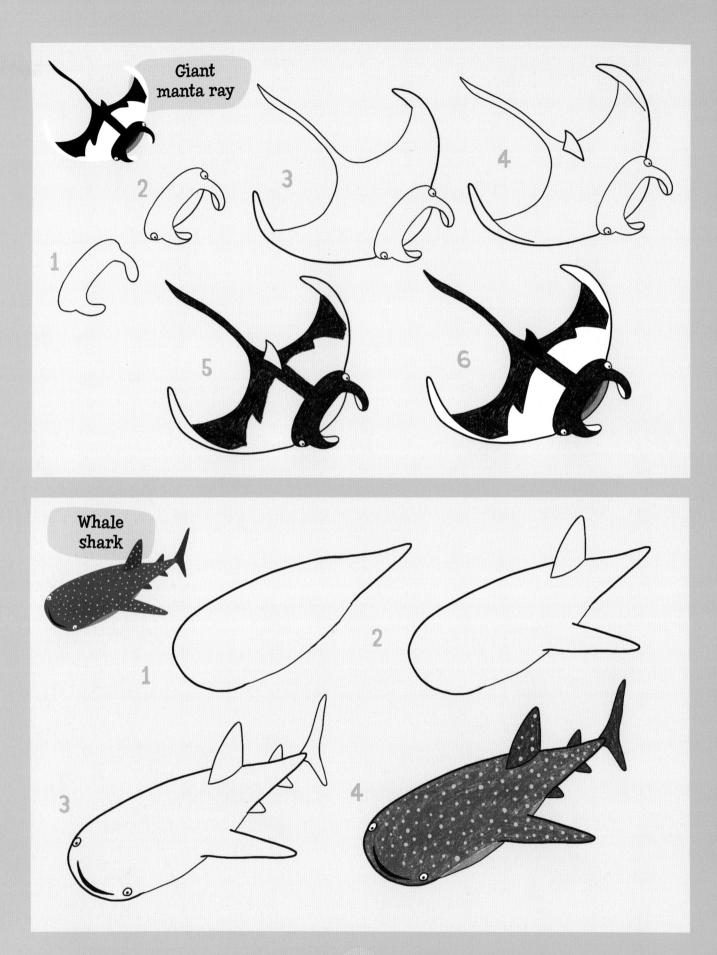

Giant manta ray

Whale shark

Black rhinoceros

1
2
3
4

Hippopotamus

1
2
3
4

Western gorilla

1

2

3

4

5

Camel

1

2

3

4

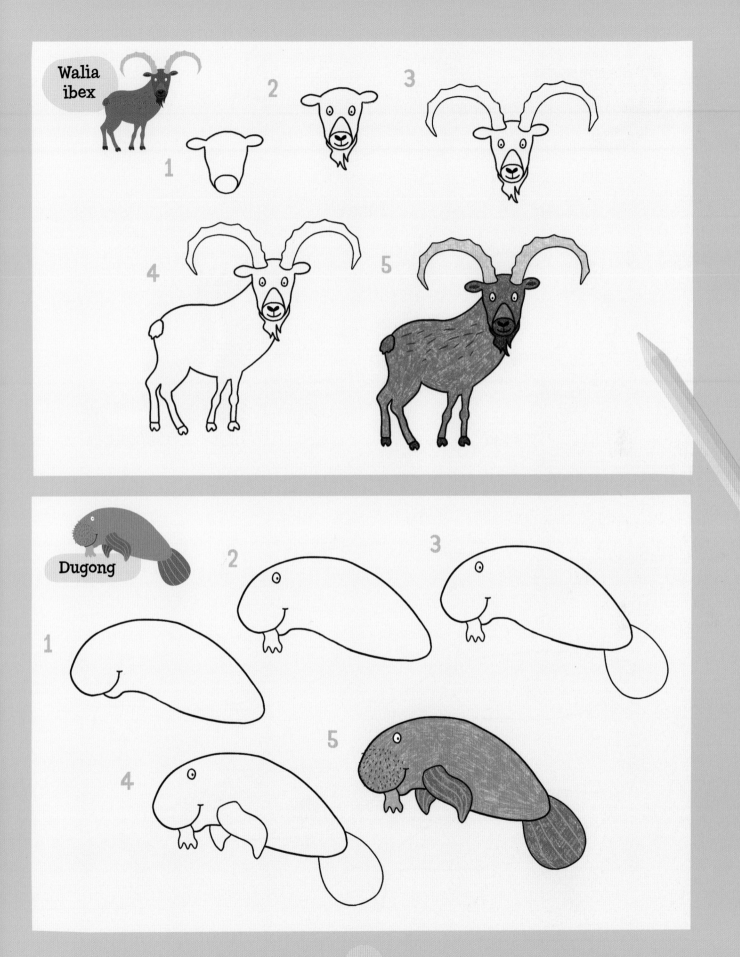

Walia ibex

1

2

3

4

5

Dugong

1

2

3

4

5

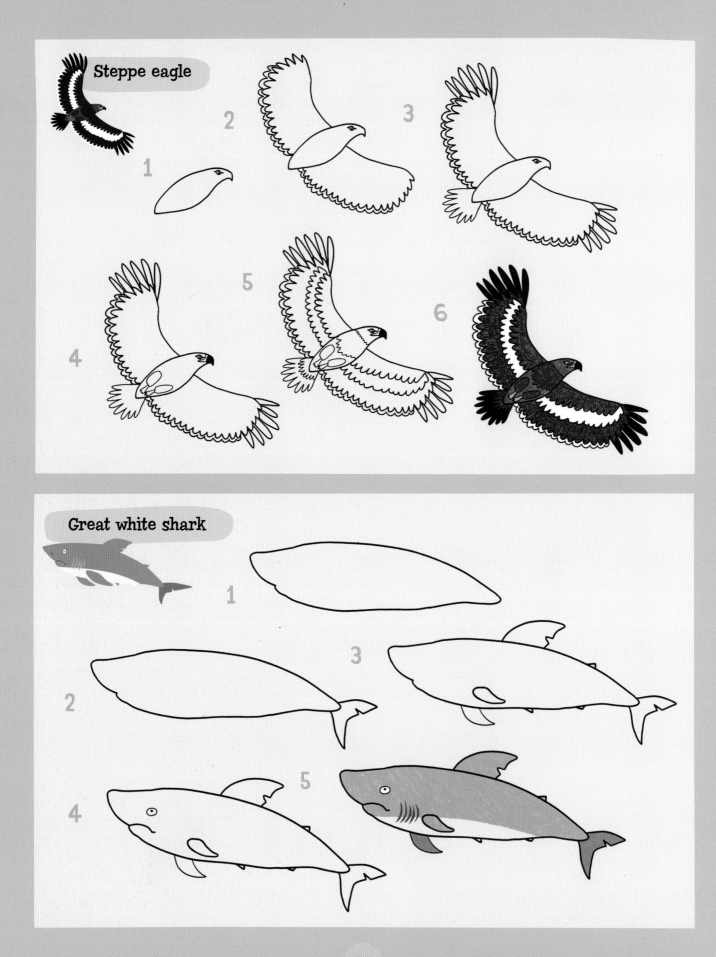

Steppe eagle

Great white shark

42

Lion

Baboon

Europe

In Europe's far north, there is polar tundra and glaciers, and at its southern edges are hot, dry scrublands. In between, there are forests, woodlands, ice-capped alps, grasslands, and sand dunes. On three sides are oceans and seas that range from freezing cold to warm. Criss-crossing the continent are many freshwater rivers.

Where in the world

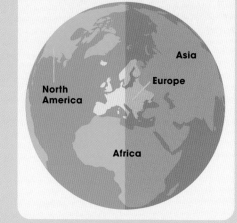

Key habitats

Sognefjord
The water in this fjord is 4,291 feet deep, and its steep, rocky sides were carved by glaciers.

Caledonian Forest
This Scottish pine forest also has wetlands, heaths, and mountain habitats. Secretive wildcats live here.

The Alps
Running through eight countries, these alpine mountains are home to 30,000 animal species.

Black Sea
This inland sea has 180 fish species and bottlenose dolphins. Lynx, bears, and wolves roam its forests.

The animals

Stag beetle
Male beetles have huge antler-like jaws! After years underground as larvae, adults emerge to live four months.

Tawny owl
These short-winged owls hunt at night in dense forests for their preferred prey of small mammals.

Red squirrel
The long, bushy tail aids squirrels' agility and balance in trees where they spend most of their time.

Camargue horse
These small, hardy white horses are an ancient breed. The wetlands of Camargue, France, is their home.

Great spotted woodpecker

When woodpeckers drum or tap tree trunks, they are searching for food, making a nest, finding a mate, or claiming territory.

Norway lobster

These lobsters only leave their sand burrow on deep ocean floors to feed at night.

Hedgehog

Hedgehogs have 5,000 spines. When scared, they roll into protective spiky balls.

Fire salamander

These 6- to 12-inch amphibians live near water in forests. They eat insects, slugs, and worms.

Common raven

Ravens are highly intelligent birds. In the wild, they can survive for more than 23 years.

Red fox

These foxes survive in almost every habitat, even cities, and eat almost anything. Their tails aid balance.

Whooper swan

Known for their "whooping" call, these swans have an eight-foot wingspan. Each bill pattern is unique.

Mediterranean monk seal

These highly endangered seals live in remote areas of coastline. They live in colonies and hunt fish, octopus, and crabs.

Hermann's tortoise

These 3- to 11-inch tortoises live in forests and scrubland, and eat leaves and flowers.

Wild boar

Closely related to the domestic pig, wild boars are nocturnal. They sleep all day and forage at night.

Badger

Badgers live in underground tunnels and chambers, called setts. A badger will eat 200 earthworms a night.

Iberian lynx

There are only 400 lynx left in the wild. Rabbits form the bulk of their diet, but they will eat ducks and young deer.

Gray wolf

These wolves mate for life and live in family groups in remote areas. A pack can bring down a moose.

White-tailed eagle

Also known as sea eagles, these three-foot-tall raptors have an eight-foot wingspan. They live near open water.

Lemming

Most lemmings are solitary, but some species can have mass migrations. They eat roots, buds, seeds, and twigs.

European eel

Adult eels live in freshwater rivers, but head to the ocean to spawn. They have a mostly marine diet.

Chamois

These goat-antelopes stand 31 inches tall. Sure-footed on steep mountainsides, they eat grasses and barks.

Common shrew

These poor-sighted rodents use their whiskers to find prey such as crickets. Their bite paralyzes their prey.

Reindeer

Some species live on the tundra, others in forests. In summer, they eat grasses and leaves. In winter, they dig in the snow for lichen.

Bottlenose dolphin

These marine mammals always appear to be smiling. They live in pods and communicate with each other.

European hare

Found in abundance in grasslands, forests, and woodlands, these fast-running hares have long ears.

Sperm whale

These toothed, large-headed whales can dive for 90 minutes. They eat a ton of fish and squid a day.

Let's learn to draw!

Mediterranean monk seal

Common raven

Red fox

Wild boar

European eel

Whooper swan

48

Red squirrel

1
2
3
4
5

Hermann's tortoise

1
2
3
4
5
6

Great spotted woodpecker

1
2
3
4
5

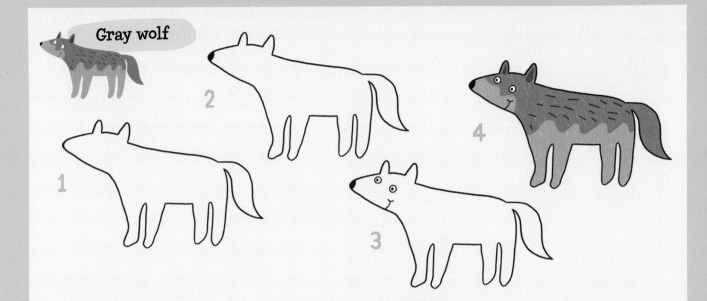

Gray wolf

1
2
3
4

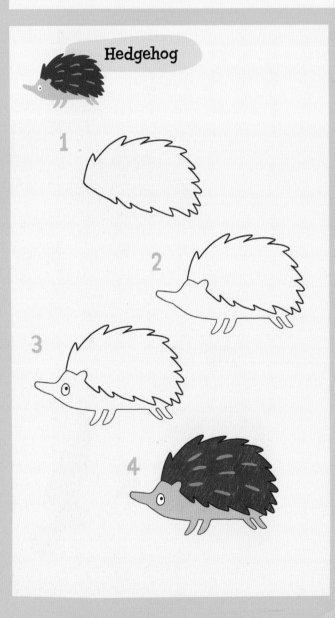

Hedgehog

1
2
3
4

Badger

1
2
3
4
5
6

Reindeer

1

2

3

4

Sperm whale

1

2

3

4

51

Tawny owl

Chamois

Bottlenose dolphin

Iberian lynx

1 2 3 4 5

European hare

1 2 3 4

Fire salamander

1 2 3 4 5

53

Norway lobster

1
2
3
4
5

Common shrew

1
2
3
4
5

Lemming

1
2
3
4

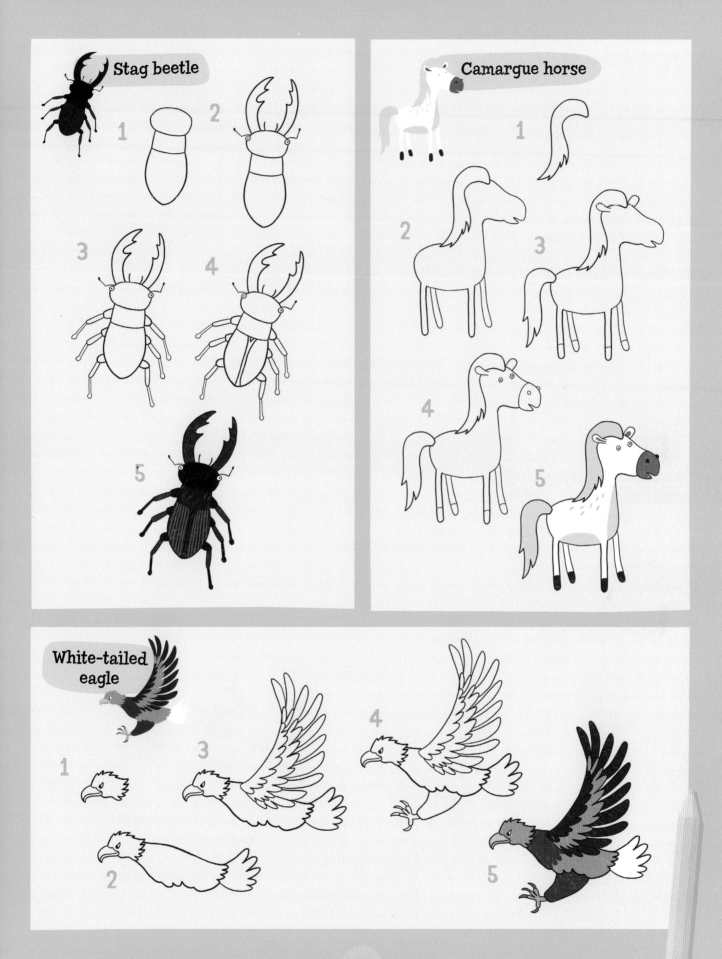

Stag beetle

Camargue horse

White-tailed eagle

Asia

The land masses and islands of Asia make up one-third of all the land on Earth. Its climate is arctic and sub-arctic in Siberia in the north, but its southern extreme is humid and tropical. Asia's deserts, mountains, plateaus, rainforests, rivers, seas, and oceans are home to incredibly diverse and unique wildlife.

Where in the world

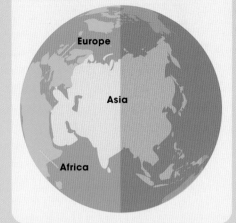

Europe

Asia

Africa

Key habitats

Gobi Desert
This vast, dry desert covers parts of Mongolia and China. Its summers are very hot and its winters freezing.

Himalayas
Containing the world's highest mountains, including Everest, its peaks are always snow-covered.

Eurasian Steppe
This dry grassland covers parts of Asia and eastern Europe. Antelopes, horses, and camels live here.

Arctic tundra
This permafrost, barren landscape is one of the harshest places for animals and plants to survive.

The animals

Red-crowned crane
These five-foot-tall cranes live in huge flocks and are regarded as sacred in Japan. They eat fish, meat, and plants.

Blue peafowl
The tail feathers of male peafowls can be raised to create a fan. Peafowls eat berries, grains, and lizards.

Asian giant hornet
These 1.8-inch hornets have three-inch wingspans. Their stinger injects a painful venom. They eat other insects.

Komodo dragon
Ten-foot-long male Komodos rear up on their hind legs to display dominance. Their bite is toxic.

Siberian tiger

These tigers are the world's largest cat. Solitary tigers roam northern forests, then lie in wait for elk and wild boar.

Orangutan

Orangutans are one of mankind's closest relatives. They spend 80 percent of their time up in rainforest trees.

Tokay gecko

Tokay geckos have "sticky" toe pads—they can climb anything and do it at lightning speed.

Giant salamander

These amphibians grow to six feet long! They live mostly in water, and eat fish, frogs, and aquatic insects.

Atlas moth

The largest of all moths have 10-inch wingspans. Adults live just two weeks as they have no mouth to ingest food.

Sika deer

Sika deer are natives of eastern Asia and Japan. They live in forests, marshes, and grasslands.

Arabian oryx

These small antelopes graze plants. Shovel-like hooves let them walk on sand.

King cobra

King cobra venom could kill an elephant! They can lift most of their 18-foot-long body upright.

Screw-horned markhor

The corkscrew-like horns can measure 63 inches on males. Markhors live in mountain forests.

Bumblebee bat

These cave-dwelling bats are just 1.3 inches long! They are the smallest mammals in the world!

Snow leopard

Snow leopards are rarely seen. They are the only big cats to survive in the cold deserts of Asia.

Giant panda

Pandas live in forests, high in the mountains. They spend up to 14 hours a day eating bamboo!

Red panda

Red pandas are about the size of a house cat. They descend from their tree dwellings head first.

Wild yak

Thick, shaggy fur protects wild yaks from the low temperatures in their habitat.

Green pheasant

Japan's national bird can sense tiny Earth tremors. They all call out when a quake is coming.

Malayan tapir

These solitary animals eat shoots and leaves in tropical forests. They can swim and hold their breath for 90 seconds.

Finless porpoise

These porpoises lack a dorsal fin. They are found in coastal waters up to 160 feet deep.

Bhutan glory

When resting and to avoid predators, these butterflies hide their colorful hindwings under their forewings.

Onager

These wild asses live in grasslands and deserts. They get most of the water they need from the grasses they eat.

Rhinoceros hornbill

These large hornbills have a decorative casque on their head. It almost looks like a second beak.

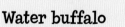

Water buffalo

These big beasts wallow in muddy water to regulate their temperature in their hot climate. They eat grasses and herbs.

Raccoon dog

Raccoon dogs can eat toxic toads! They produce lots of saliva that dilutes the toxins.

Japanese macaque

Also known as snow monkeys, they are great swimmers and are known to soak for ages in hot springs.

Sand grouse
Because these game birds live in dry habitats, males carry water to the nests in their feathers.

Jerboa
Jerboas are desert rodents that hop around like tiny kangaroos. Their hind legs are four times longer than their front legs.

Bengal tiger
The stripes on each big cat are unique. Stealth and camouflage make them excellent hunters.

Japanese spider crab
The legspan of these crabs is 13 feet! For camouflage, they cover their shells with seaweed.

Camel spider
The jaws on these six-inch-long arachnids can measure two inches. They are fierce predators that hunt small birds, insects, and rodents.

Colugo
These tree-dwelling mammals glide by extending folds of skin between their limbs.

Slow loris
Extra-large eyes give lorises excellent night vision. They sleep, curled in a ball, in trees.

Baikal seal
These seals are found at Lake Baikal in Russia. They are the only freshwater seals in the world.

Sand cat
The paws of desert cats have a special covering so they can walk on the sand and not leave any pawprints behind.

Spotted seal
These silvery gray seals eat a variety of fish. They dive to depths of 1,000 feet when hunting.

Asian elephant
The ears of this elephant are smaller and rounder than those of African elephants. They eat 300 pounds of vegetation a day.

Let's learn to draw!

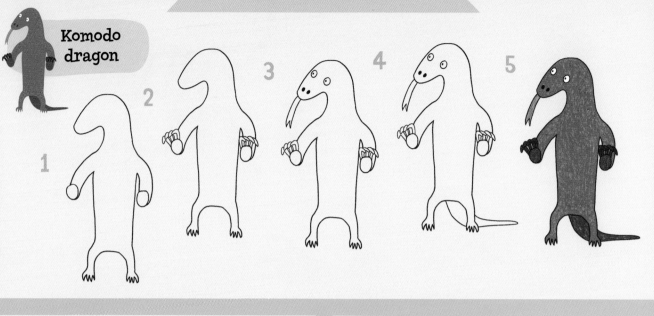

Komodo dragon

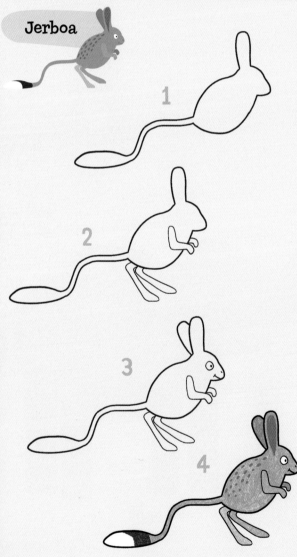

Jerboa

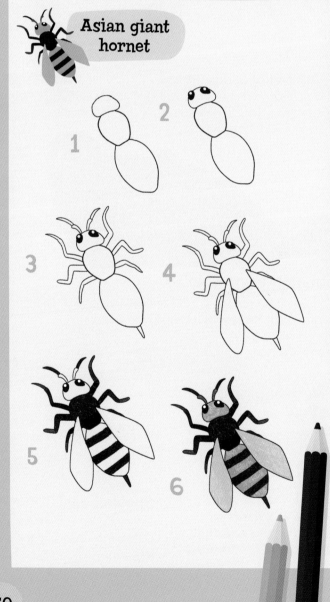

Asian giant hornet

Giant panda

1

2

3

4

5

Asian elephant

1

2

3

4

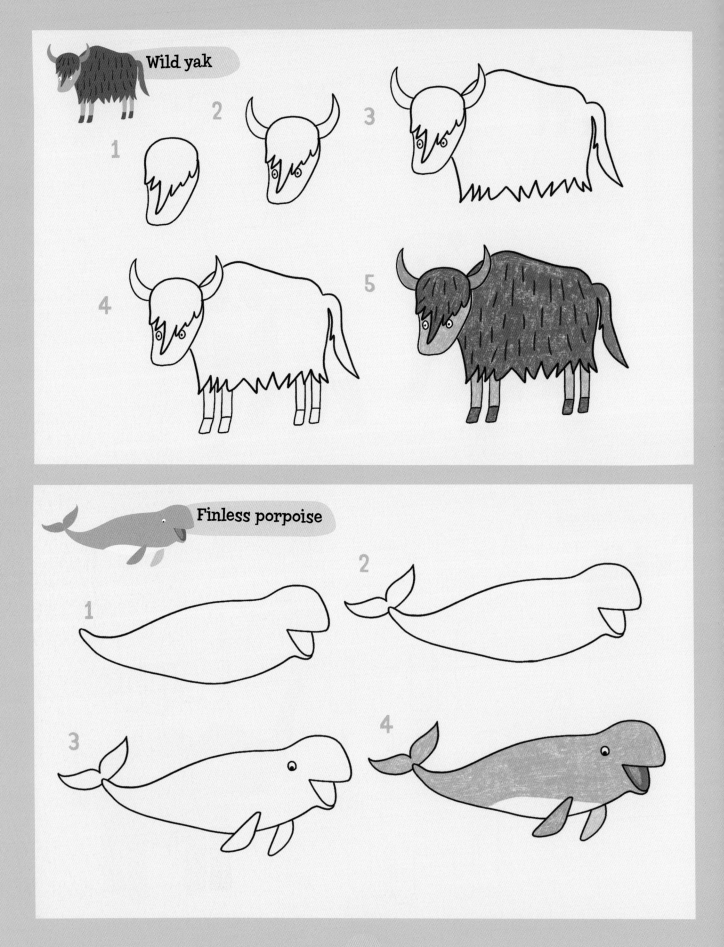

Wild yak

Finless porpoise

Screw-horned markhor

1
2
3
4
5
6

Colugo

1
2
3
4
5

Bhutan glory

1
2
3
4
5

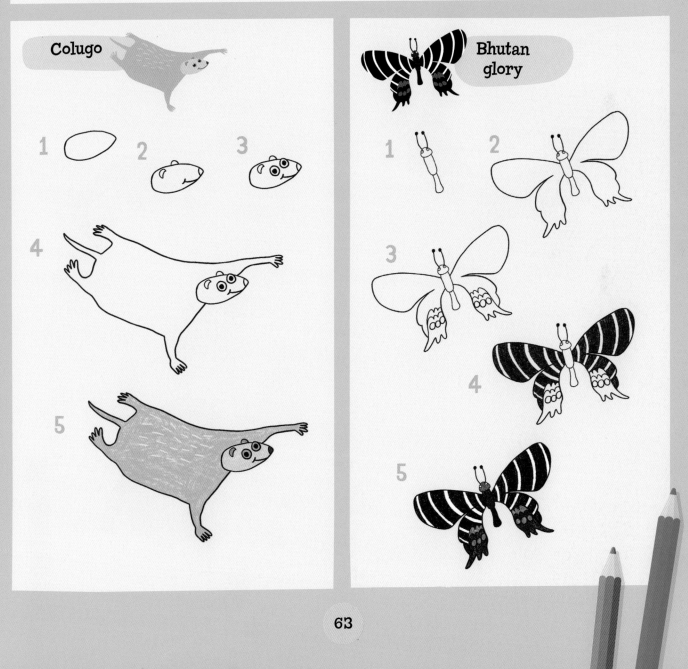

Bumblebee bat

Tokay gecko

Orangutan

Atlas moth

1

2

3

4

5

Raccoon dog

1

2

3

4

Sand grouse

1

2

3

4

Blue peafowl

1
2
3
4
5
6

Bengal tiger

1
2
3
4
5

66

Water buffalo

Red-crowned crane

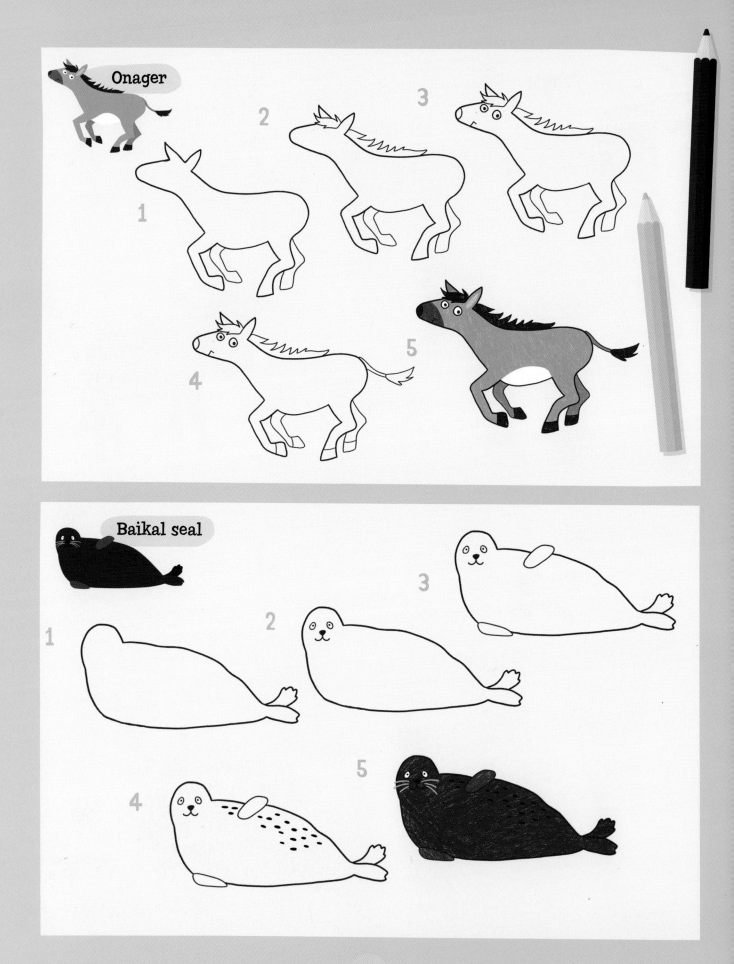

Onager

Baikal seal

Arabian oryx

Siberian tiger

Japanese macaque

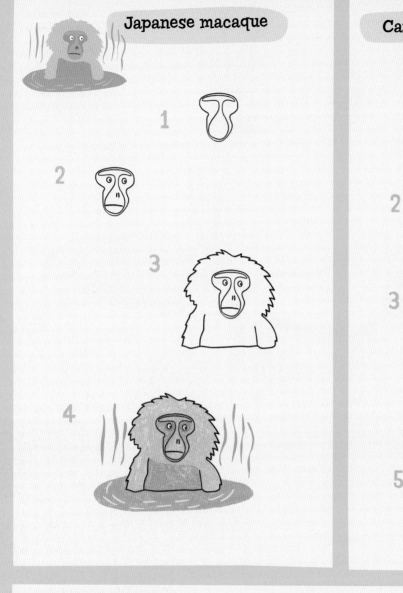

1

2

3

4

Camel spider

1

2

3

4

5

Snow leopard

1

2

3

Sika deer

Japanese spider crab

71

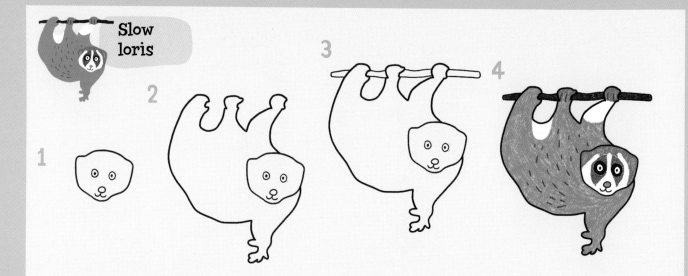

Slow loris

1

2

3

4

Sand cat

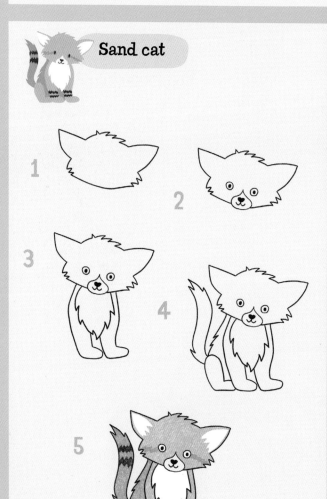

1

2

3

4

5

Giant salamander

1

2

3

Rhinoceros hornbill

King cobra

Green pheasant

73

Red panda

1

2

3

4

Spotted seal

1

2

3

4

Malayan tapir

1

2

3

4

5

74

Oceania

More than 10,000 islands make up Oceania, with Australia being the largest. Oceania has diverse habitats: arid deserts, lush rainforests, woody forests, tropical beaches, mangroves, and even glaciers. Many animals of Oceania, like koalas, kangaroos, platypuses, and cassowaries, are found nowhere else on the planet.

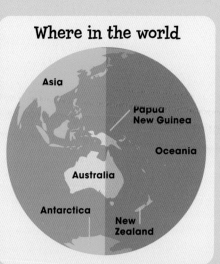

Where in the world

Asia

Papua New Guinea

Oceania

Australia

Antarctica

New Zealand

Key habitats

Great Barrier Reef
This string of coral reefs contains 400 types of coral, 1,500 fish species, and 4,000 types of mollusks.

Australian outback
Australia's interior has rocky plains, grasslands, deserts, salt pans, and scrublands. Monsoons are frequent.

Fiordland
This New Zealand national park is famed for its glacier-carved fjords. There are forests, ferns, and mosses.

Polynesia
Wet, tropical habitats dominate the more than 1,000 Pacific Ocean islands of Polynesia.

The animals

Possum
These nocturnal marsupials eat leaves, flowers, fruits, insects, bird's eggs, and baby birds.

Wallaby
These marsupials are smaller than kangaroos. Wallaby joeys are born early and carried in a pouch.

Quokka
These 16- to 21-inch-long marsupials often look like they're smiling. They eat grass, leaves, stems, and bark.

Emu
Emus are the world's second-largest bird. They can run at 31 mph, using their wings to steer.

Koala

Koalas are marsupials and eat only eucalyptus leaves. They sleep in trees for 18 to 22 hours a day.

Red kangaroo

The strong hind legs of kangaroos propel leaps of 25 feet long and six feet high. They eat green plants, and most live in mobs of 10.

Platypus

Platypuses lay eggs and feed their young milk. They live in water and nest on land. The males have venomous ankle spurs.

Kiwi

These flightless birds are native to New Zealand. They are the only birds with nostrils at the end of their beak.

Bilby

These rabbit-sized marsupials have huge ears and a long snout. They extract water from the plants they eat.

Yellow-crested cockatoo

These noisy parrots live in tropical forests feeding on seeds, fruits, and flowers. They mate for life.

Rainbow lorikeet

These colorful parrots eat fruit, pollen, and nectar, which is collected on their bristle-tipped tongue.

Little penguin

Standing 12 inches high, little penguins have blue and white feathers, and spend four-fifths of their lives in the sea.

Hairy-nosed wombat

Wombats dig tunnels 100 feet long. They are marsupials and feed on grasses, herbs, bark, and roots.

Yellow-eyed penguin

These birds are only found in coastal New Zealand forests and scrublands. They feed on fish, squid, and shellfish.

Spectacled porpoise

Rarely seen spectacled porpoises eat shrimp and anchovies. They are fast swimmers that live in groups in Antarctic waters.

Clownfish

A special mucus protects clownfish from the toxic tentacles of their anemone hosts.

Funnel-web spider

The poison of these spiders can kill a human if a bite is left untreated. Their fangs can bite through shoe leather!

Frill-necked lizard

Ruffs of skin around their necks extend when these reptiles are alarmed. This makes them look larger.

Tuatara

Tuataras live in coastal forests and scrublands. Crests line their spine, and they can live to 100 years old!

Long-beaked echidna

New Guinea's spiny long-beaked echidnas lay eggs and produce milk for their young.

Kakapo

These nocturnal, flightless forest parrots are vegetarians. There are only several hundred individuals of this species left.

Dingo

These wild dogs live in packs headed by a dominant male and female. They eat fruit and grains if meat is not available.

Kookaburra

These birds have a "laughing" call. They seize worms, crustaceans, and insects with their four-inch beaks.

Water-holding frog

After living below ground for years, these frogs emerge after rain to feed and build up fat and water reserves.

Cassowary

When threatened, these large, flightless birds head-butt predators with the casque atop their heads.

Tasmanian devil

These dog-sized marsupials are found in Tasmania. They growl and screech, and have a powerful bite.

Weedy seadragon

Weedy seadragons have leaf-like structures that camouflage them among their kelp frond habitat.

Let's learn to draw!

Platypus

Kookaburra

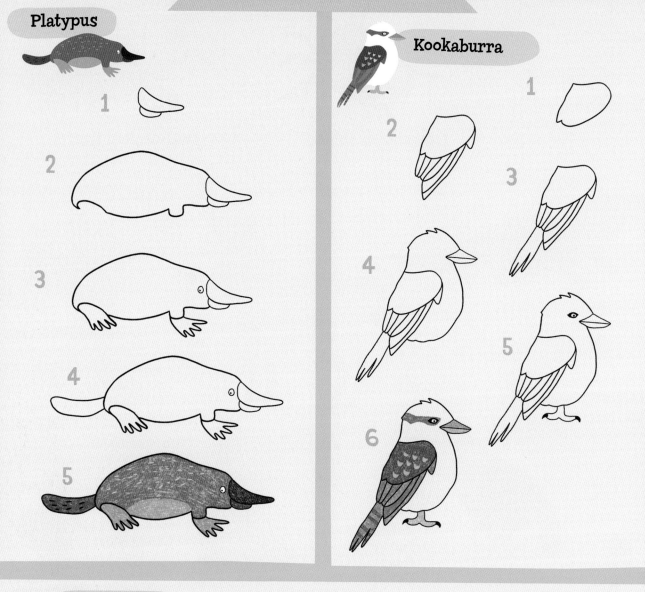

Water-holding frog

78

Cassowary

Red kangaroo

79

Koala

1   2   3

4   5   6

Spectacled porpoise

1   2

3

Kakapo

Tasmanian devil

Emu

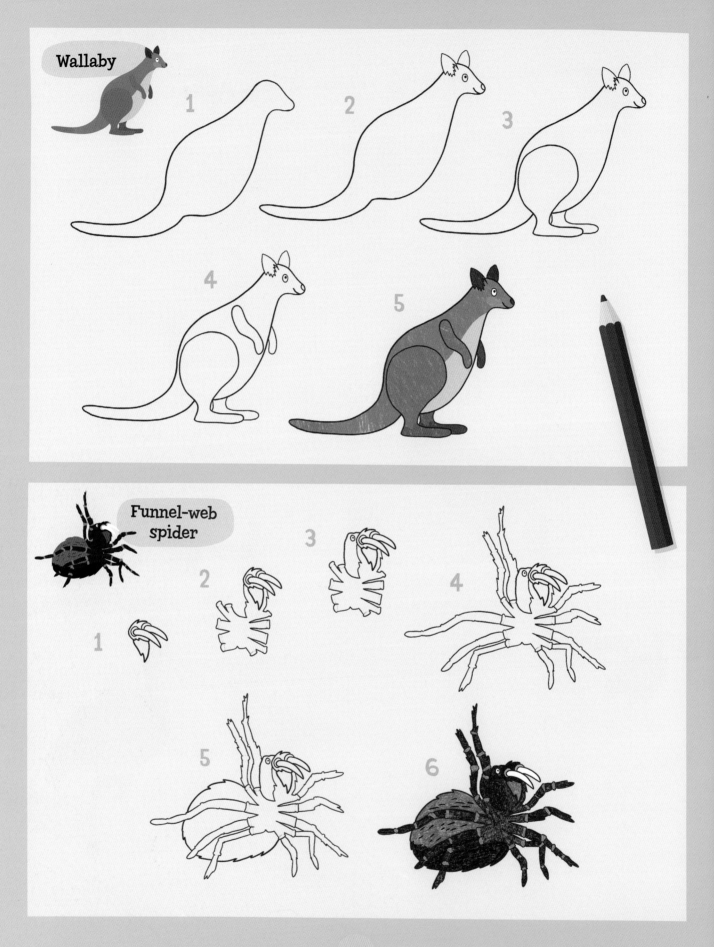

Wallaby

1

2

3

4

5

Funnel-web spider

1

2

3

4

5

6

Quokka

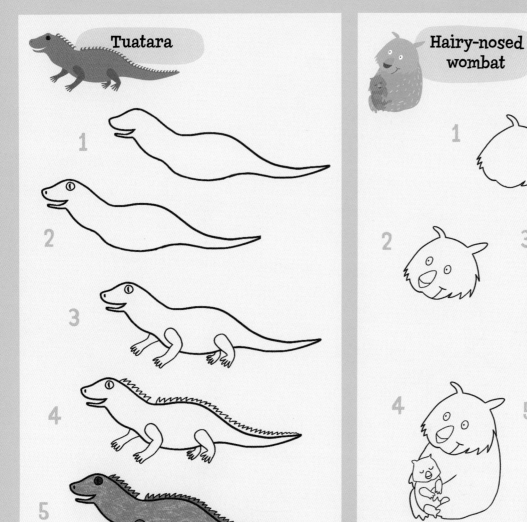

Tuatara

Hairy-nosed wombat

Rainbow lorikeet

1   2   3   4

Bilby

1   2   3   4   5

Yellow-crested cockatoo

1   2   3   4   5

Dingo

Frill-necked lizard

Long-beaked echidna

Clownfish

1

2

3

4

Possum

1

2

3

4

5

Little penguin

1

2

3

4

86

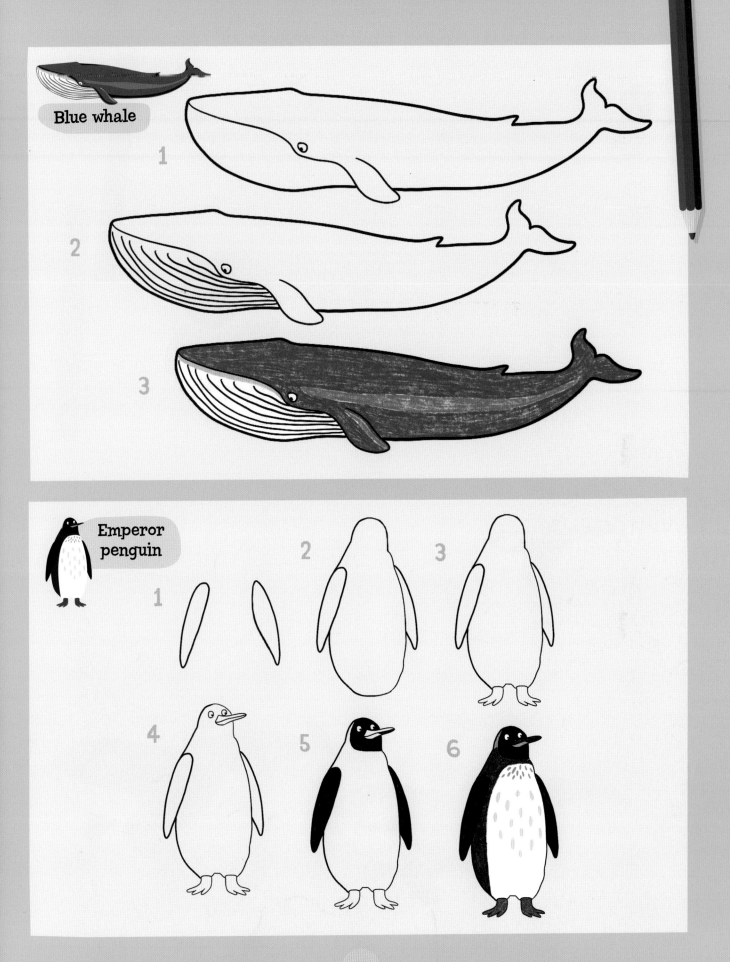

Blue whale

1

2

3

Emperor penguin

1

2

3

4

5

6

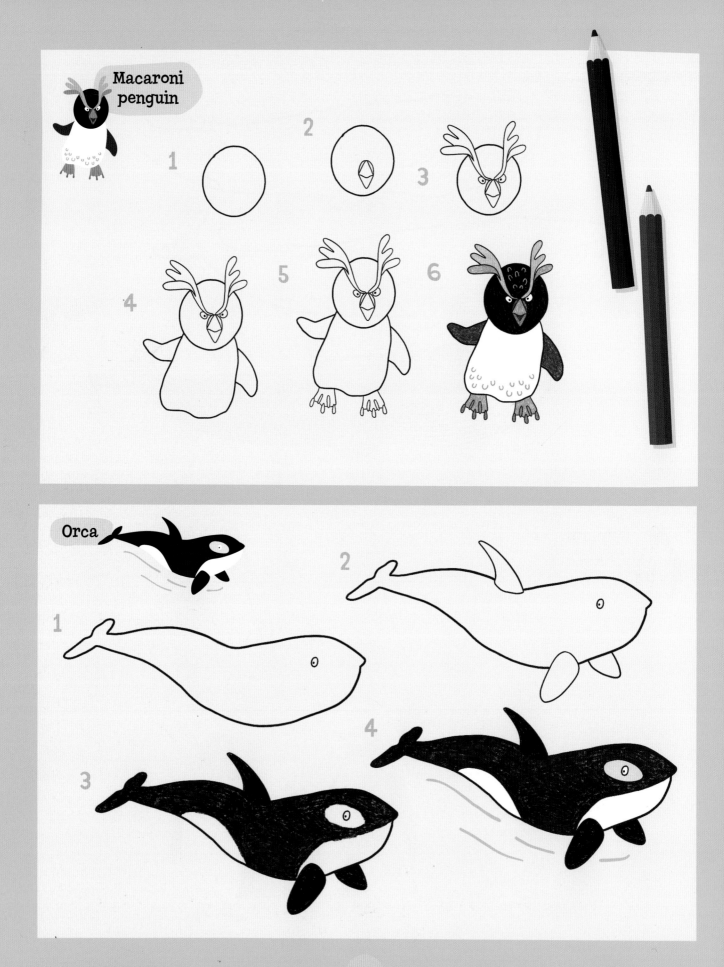

Macaroni penguin

1 2 3

4 5 6

Orca

1 2

3 4

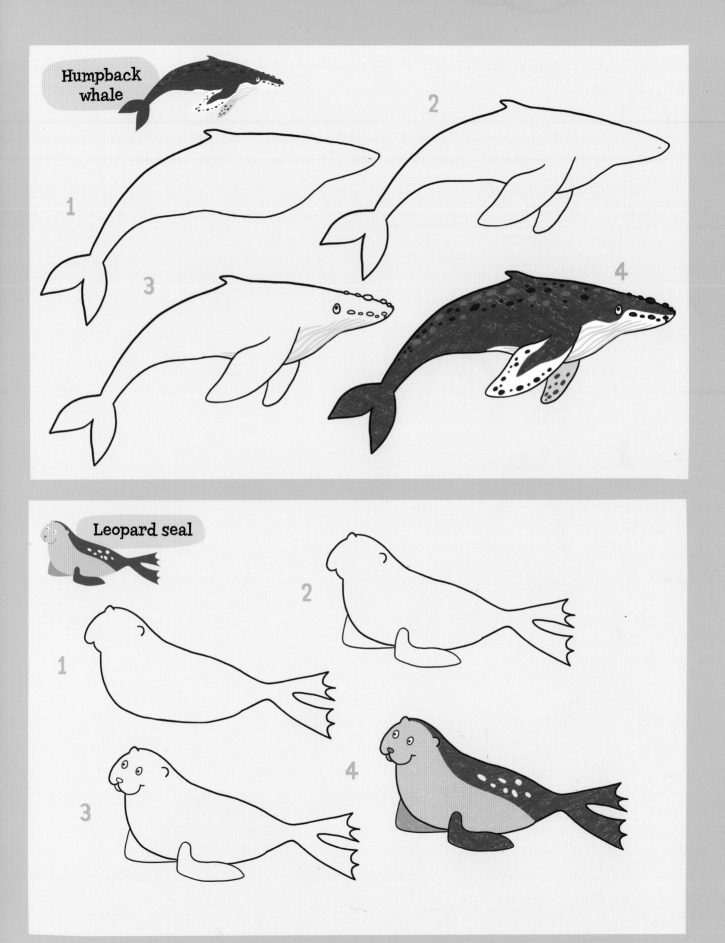

Humpback whale

1

2

3

4

Leopard seal

1

2

3

4

Chinstrap penguin

1
2
3
4
5

Arctic tern

1
2
3
4
5

Weddell seal

1
2
3
4

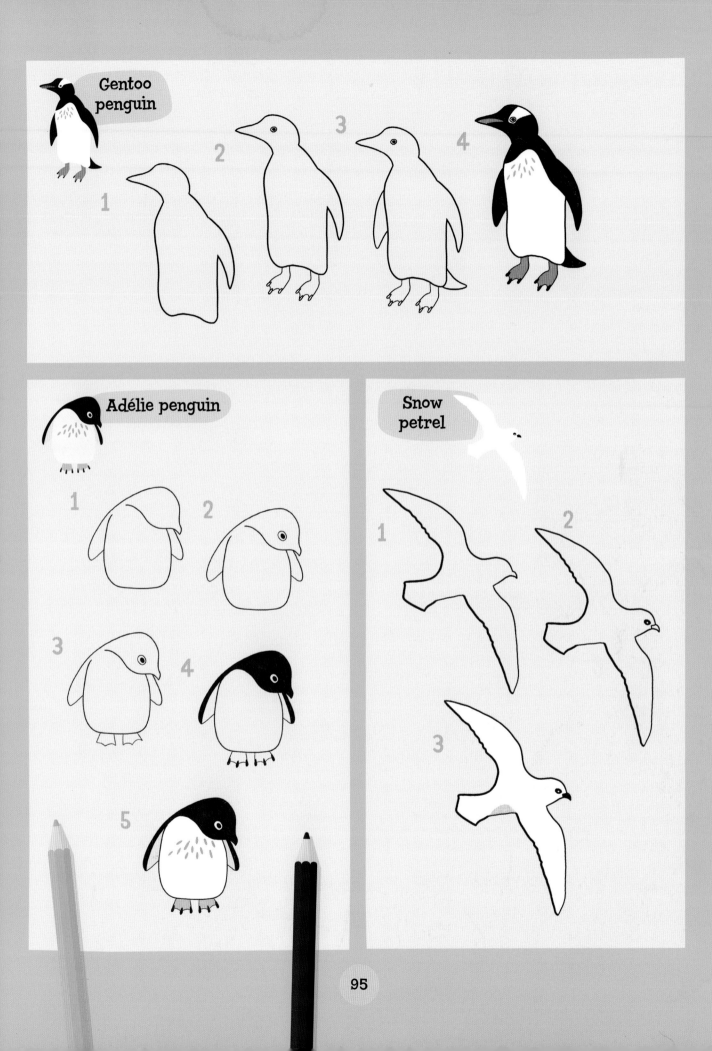

Gentoo penguin

1 2 3 4

Adélie penguin

1 2 3 4 5

Snow petrel

1 2 3

95

Index of animals

Weedy seadragon

1

2

3

4

Kiwi

1

2

3

4

Yellow-eyed penguin

1

2

3

4

Antarctica

Antarctica is the most southernly region on the planet and is an enormous ice-covered continent surrounded by the Southern Ocean. It is Earth's coldest place, but its low rainfall makes it a desert. Only specially adapted plants and animals survive this harsh environment. Just a few species live here year-round; most visit to feed or breed.

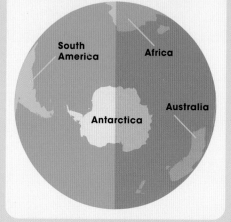

Where in the world

South America

Africa

Australia

Antarctica

Key habitats

Peninsula and coasts

Plants and animals visit and live only around the warmer, mostly ice-free, edges of this continent.

Southern Ocean

During winter, over half of this ocean is covered in icebergs. It is rich in plant and animal life.

Halley Bay

Until 2016, a huge emperor penguin rookery was here. But global climate change has caused the ice to break up.

Bird Island

Tens of thousands of birds live or breed here, and whales feed on the krill in the surrounding waters.

The animals

Wandering albatross

Their record-breaking wingspan is 11 feet. They can glide for several hours without flapping their wings.

Chinstrap penguin

Chinstrap penguins breed in colonies of 100,000 pairs. Their diet includes krill, small fish, and crustaceans.

Leopard seal

Don't be fooled by their smiley expressions. These aggressive predators feed on penguins and young seals.

Emperor penguin

Standing 45 inches tall, these are the largest penguins. They can dive to 1,850 feet and stay under water for 20 minutes.

Humpback whale

Humpback whales visit Antarctica during the summer months to feast on Antarctic krill.

Arctic tern

These terns fly from their Arctic breeding grounds to the Antarctic each year—a 22,000-mile round trip.

Blue whale

Blue whales are the largest animals on Earth. They grow to 105 feet long and weigh 200 tons.

Snow petrel

Snow petrels are one of only three bird species that breed on Antarctica. They run on the water to take off.

Gentoo penguin

Gentoos build nests with stones, feathers, grass, and sticks. Both parents care for their young.

Orca

Orcas are a dolphin species and grow to nine-feet long. They don't migrate, but follow where food is available in cooler waters.

Macaroni penguin

Unlike most other penguins that waddle, macaroni penguins hop to get around on land!

Adélie penguin

These are the smallest Antarctic penguin and like the emperor they live and breed only on Antarctica.

Antarctic krill

These 2.5-inch crustaceans are the main food of whales and many other animals. A cubic yard of water can contain 10,000 krill.

Weddell seal

These seals dive below the ice to hunt for food. They create holes in the ice to breathe through.

Let's learn to draw!

Antarctic krill

Arctic O[cean]

Alaska

Greenland

Iceland

Europe

North
America

Hawaii

Atlantic
Ocean

Africa

The Caribbean

Pacific
Ocean

Central
America

Galapagos
Islands

South
America

This world map shows where
the animals can be found,
but it does not show global
or seasonal distribution.

Falkland
Islands

Southern O[cean]

South America

ain lion

Blue morpho
butterfly

Emerald tree boa

Jaguar

Galapagos
penguin

Flying
tree frog

Sloth

Chimpanzee

Gila monster

Poison dart
frog

Giant armadillo

Galapagos
giant tortoise

Pudu

Dung beetle

Ostrich

arwhal

Andean
condor

Ring-tailed lemur

Zebra

Toucan

Flamingo

Magnificent
frigatebird

Chameleon

Giraffe

eagle

Giant anteater

Camel

Mudskipper

Giant manta ray

Hippopotamus

Western gorilla

Llama

Piranha

Steppe
eagle

Africa

nere

Whale
shark

Caracal

Baboon

Walia ibex

Leopard

Goliath frog

Giant African
land snail

mals

ve

African elephant

Great white shark

Horned desert
viper

Dugong

Lion

Black rhinoceros

Sperm
whale

Reindeer

Bottlenose
dolphin

European hare

Whooper
swan

Common shrew

Raven

Norway
lobster

Lemming

Europe

Red fox

Blue peafowl

Wild boar

Red
squirrel

Gray wolf

Great spotted
woodpecker

Stag
beetle

Chamois

Giant salamander

Red panda

Hedgehog

Iberian lynx

Camargue
horse

que   Onager

Arabian oryx

Rhinoceros
hornbill

Badger

White-tailed
eagle

Asia

Slow loris

Malayan tapir

European
eel

Tawny
owl

Raccoon dog

Colugo

Komodo
dragon

Sika deer

Sand grouse

Hermann's
tortoise

Mediterranean
monk seal

eopard   Bengal Tiger

Wild yak

Finless porpoise

Sand cat

Red-crowned
crane

Baikal seal

Fire salamander